The Five Senses

Using Your Senses

Rebecca Rissman

www.capstonepub.com
Visit our website to find out more information about Heinemann-Raintree books.

To order:
 Phone 800-747-4992
Visit www.capstonepub.com to browse our catalog and order online.

Edited by Rebecca Rissman, Daniel Nunn, and Harriet Milles
Designed by Joanna Hinton-Malivoire
Picture research by Tracy Cummins
Originated by Capstone Global Library Ltd.
Production by Victoria Fitzgerald

102014
008579R

Library of Congress Cataloging-in-Publication Data
Rissman, Rebecca.

Using your senses / Rebecca Rissman.
    p. cm.
Originally published: 2010.
Includes bibliographical references and index.
ISBN 978-1-4329-5350-8 (hc)—ISBN 978-1-4329-5495-6 (pb) 1.
Senses and sensation—Juvenile literature. I. Title.
QP434.R57 2012
612.8—dc22   2010045846

Acknowledgments
The author and publishers are grateful to the following for permission to reproduce copyright material: ageFOTOSTOCK: John Birdsall, 20; Alamy: PhotoAlto, cover bottom right; Getty Images: altrendo images, 6, Jens Koenig, 15 right, Paul Conrath, 16, Peter Adams, 13 left; iStockphoto: Katrina Brown, 19, Linda Kloosterhof, cover middle, 18, Sean Locke, 4, Tyler Stalman, 12; Shutterstock: Andy Lim, 8, Ben Smith, 5 left, BestPhoto1, cover top right, Bryan Sikora, 17 left, clickit, 11 left, Felix Mizioznikov, 10, Gravicapa, cover top left, Jhaz Photography, 11 right, Katrina Brown, back cover, 9 left, Margarita Borodina, 13 right, Muellek, 14, prism68, 21, Richard Clark, 9 right, s_oleg, 5 right, Studio 1One, cover bottom left, 5 middle, Supri Suharjoto, 17 right, Victor Newman, 7, wavebreakmedia ltd, 15 left

We would like to thank Dr. Matt Siegel for his invaluable help in the preparation of this book.

Every effort has been made to contact copyright holders of any material reproduced in this book. Any omissions will be rectified in subsequent printings if notice is given to the publisher.

Some words appear in bold, **like this**. You can find out what they mean in "Words to Know" on page 23.

Contents

About this series

Books in this series introduce readers to the five senses and their associated sensory organs. Use this book to stimulate discussion about how people use all of their senses to understand the world around them.

Your Sensory System

People have five **senses**. Senses are what we use to learn about the world around us. The five senses are hearing, smelling, seeing, touching, and tasting.

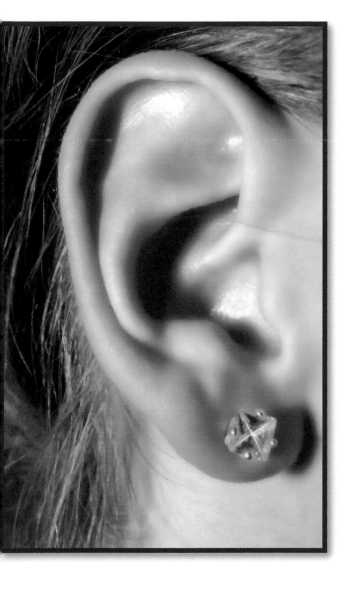  

The **sensory system** is made of different parts of your body. Different body parts help you sense things. Together, these body parts make up your sensory system.

Some parts of the **sensory system** are on the outside of your body. Your ears, eyes, nose, mouth, and skin are part of the sensory system.

tongue

Some parts of the sensory system are on the inside of your body. Your **brain** is part of the sensory system. Your tongue is part of the sensory system, too.

Seeing

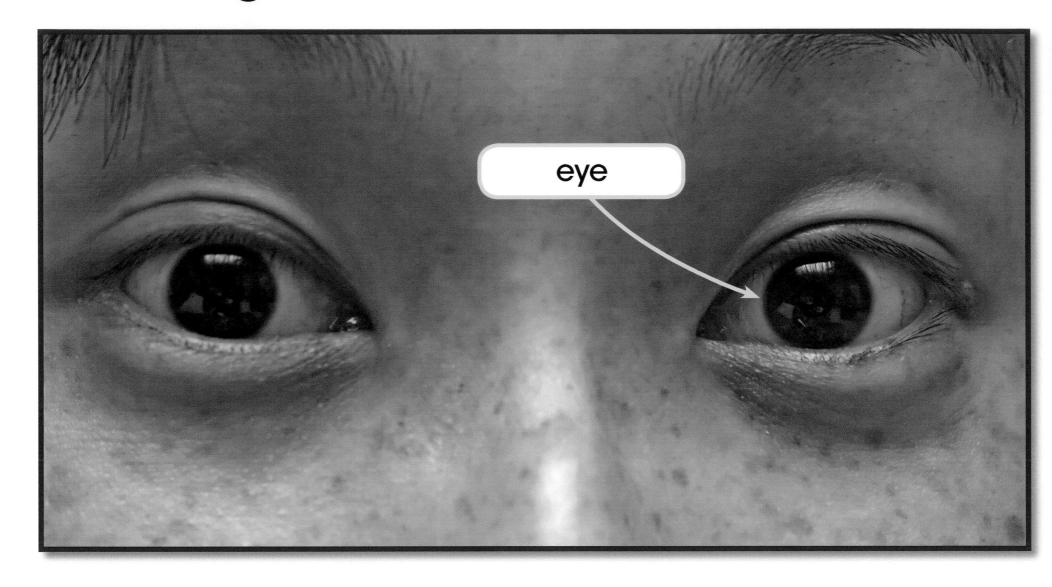

eye

You use your eyes to see things. Your eyes are in your head. Your eyes send messages to your **brain**. Your brain tells you what you are seeing.

Your eyes can see different colors and shapes. Your eyes can see if something is moving or still. What else can your eyes see?

Hearing

ear

You use your ears to hear sounds. Your ears are on your head. Your ears send messages to your **brain**. Your brain tells you what you are hearing.

Your ears can hear loud and quiet sounds. Your ears can hear high sounds, such as a bird singing. Your ears can hear low sounds, such as thunder. What else can your ears hear?

Tasting

nose

tongue

You use your tongue and nose to **sense flavors**. Your tongue is in your mouth. Your nose is on your head. Your tongue and nose send messages to your **brain**. Your brain tells you how your food tastes.

You can taste different flavors. Your tongue can taste spicy food. Your tongue can taste sweet fruit. What else can your tongue taste?

Smelling

nose

You use your nose to smell **scents**. Your nose is on your head. Your nose sends messages to your **brain**. Your brain tells you what you are smelling.

You can smell many different scents. Your nose can smell food. Your nose can smell flowers. What else can your nose smell?

Touching

skin

You use your skin to touch things. Your skin is on the outside of your body. **Nerves** under your skin send messages to your **brain**. Your brain tells you what you are touching.

You can feel different things. You can feel rough and smooth things. You can feel hot and cold things. What else can you feel?

Using Your Senses

You use your **senses** every day. You use your senses of feeling, tasting, and smelling to help you to eat.

You use your senses to get around. You use your senses of touching and seeing to walk and run.

hearing aid

Many people use their **sense** of hearing to **communicate**. But some people cannot hear well. They may use their hands to spell out **sign language**. They may wear a **hearing aid**.

Braille

Many people use their sense of seeing to read. But some people cannot see. They may use their sense of touch to read. They may read in **Braille**.

Can You Remember?

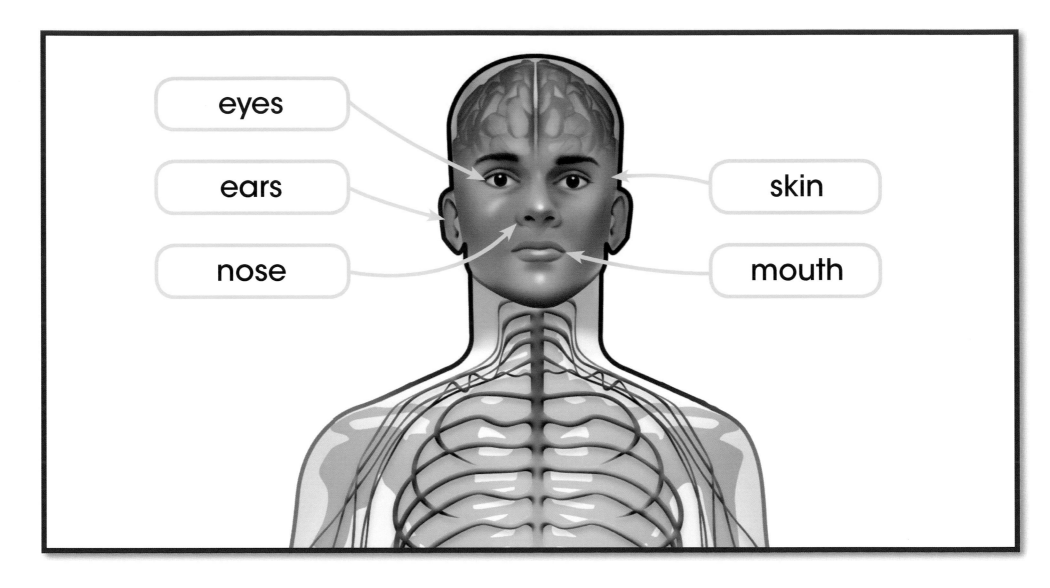

eyes

ears

nose

skin

mouth

Which parts of your body do you use for tasting, seeing, smelling, hearing, and touching?

Answers on page 24

Words to Know

Braille special raised bumps on paper that make words. People read Braille with their fingers.

brain part of your body that helps you think, remember, feel, and move

communicate talk with someone else

flavor the taste and smell that something has

hearing aid small machine that helps people hear. Hearing aids fit inside and behind the ear.

nerves nerves carry messages about feelings and movements between your brain and other parts of your body

scent smell of something

sense something that helps you smell, see, touch, taste, and hear things around you

sensory system parts of your body that help you to understand the world around you. The sensory system includes your eyes, ears, nose, mouth, skin, brain, and nerves.

sign language way to communicate with hand signs

Index

Answers to questions on page 22:
You use your nose and mouth for tasting, your eyes for seeing, your nose for smelling, your ears for hearing, and your skin for touching things.

Note to Parents and Teachers

Before reading

Show the children the front cover of the book. Ask them what they know about senses. Explain to the children that people have five senses, and senses are what we use to learn about the world around us.

After reading

• Tell the children that they are going to use all of their five senses. Show the children a bowl of apples. Ask them, "Which sense are you using to look at these apples?" Then tell them to close their eyes, and ask them, "If you couldn't see the apples, what other senses could you use?" Cut up the apples so that each child has a piece to eat. Before they take a bite, ask, "When you bite into the apple, can you hear anything?" Then ask them to taste the apples. Finally ask them write about how they have used all their five senses.